D0718053

BEDFORD.

COUNTRIES

India

Ruth Thomson

WAYLAND

Explore the world with **Popcorn** - your complete first non-fiction library.

Look out for more titles in the Popcorn range. All books have the same format of simple text and striking images. Text is carefully matched to the pictures to help readers to identify and understand key vocabulary.
www.waylandbooks.co.uk/popcorn

First published in 2010 by Wayland

Wayland
Hachette Children's Books
338 Euston Road
London NW1 3BH

Wayland Australia
Level 17/207 Kent Street
Sydney NSW 2000

Produced for Wayland by
White-Thomson Publishing Ltd
www.wtpub.co.uk
+44 (0)843 208 7460

Editor: Steve White-Thomson
Designer: Amy Sparks
Picture researchers: Ruth Thomson/Steve White-Thomson
Series consultant: Kate Ruttle
Design concept: Paul Cherrill

British Library Cataloging in Publication Data
Thomson, Ruth, 1949-

India -- (Countries)(Popcorn)
1. India--Juvenile literature
I. Title II. Series
915.4-dc22

ISBN: 978 0 7502 6306 1

Wayland is a division of Hachette Children's Books,
an Hachette UK company.
www.hachette.co.uk

Printed and bound in China

Picture Credits:
Corbis: Richard Powers front cover, Jon Hicks 5; Steve Raymer/National Geographic Society 14; Photolibrary: Amit Somvanshi 17, John Henry Claude Wilson 19; Neil Thomson 23b; Shutterstock: Vishal Shah 1/9, oksana perkins 2/6r, 13, Sam DCruz 6l, 18, Igor Plotnikov 7, Luciano Mortula 8, Socrates 10, 15, Dana Ward 11, Jeremy Richards 16, 20, Ghaint 21, Darrenp 23t, Emjay Smith 23m

Contents

Where is India?

Here is a map of India.

India is a huge country in Asia.

New Delhi is the capital city.

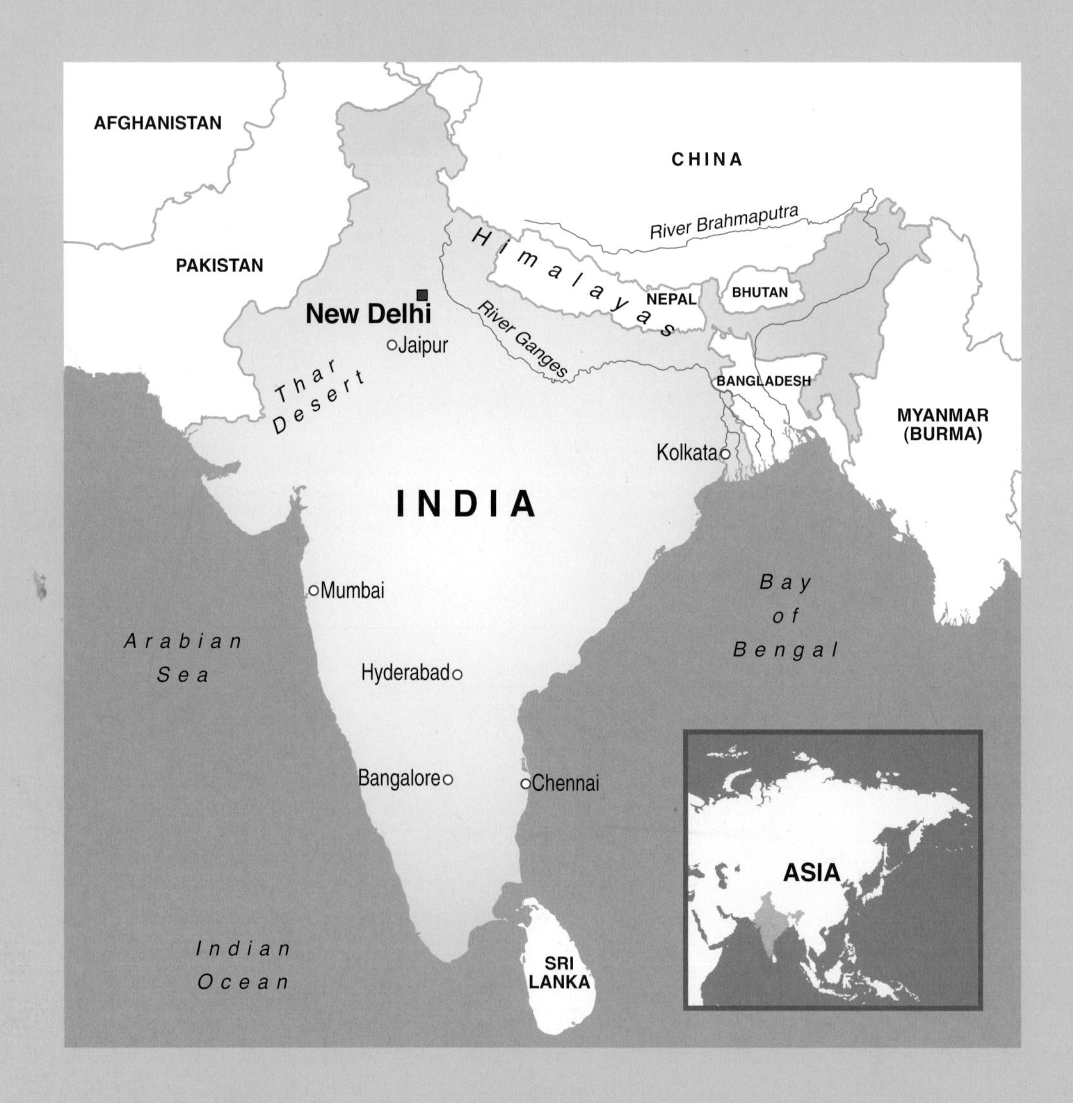

There are enormous cities in India.
These were built hundreds of years ago.
Some still have old forts and palaces.

Bangalore has many modern buildings.
Factories here make computers and aircraft parts.

Land and sea

India has high mountains, called the Himalayas, in the north. Further south, there are fertile plains, long rivers and cool hills. There is a desert in the west.

The Himalayas are the highest mountains in the world.

The desert is hot and dry. It hardly ever rains there.

India has thousands of miles of coastline. The beaches are mainly sandy. In the south, palm trees grow near to the shore.

Some fishermen live in villages on the beach. They build their own houses.

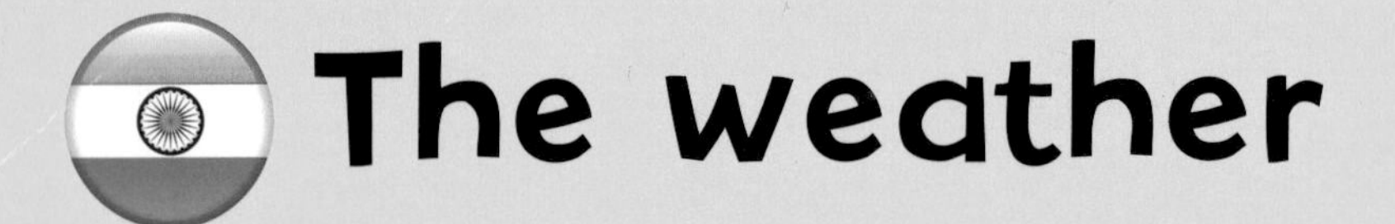

The weather

India has three seasons.

Summers are hot and dry.

It is coolest in the hills.

The air is very dusty in the summer months.

After summer, monsoon winds bring heavy rain for several months. Winters are cool. It snows in the mountains.

During the monsoon season, it rains every day.

Farmers plant rice by hand after the monsoon rains have softened the earth.

Town and country

Indian cities are very busy. The streets are full of motorbikes, autorickshaws and buses, as well as shoppers and street traders. Cows often wander the streets, too.

Cows are seen as holy animals. No-one is allowed to harm them.

autorickshaw

Many Indians live in villages.
They grow food crops. Farmers
on the plains grow wheat and rice.
Farmers in the hills grow coffee or tea.

Tea pickers pluck only the very tips of tea bushes.

Homes

More and more Indians want to live in towns and cities. They hope for a better life there. Some Indians live in smart houses. But the poorest people live in homemade shacks.

The city of Mumbai is home to 14 million people.

Many village houses do not have running water or electricity. Women collect water from a well and wash clothes in rivers. They cook on stoves outside.

People use wood or cow dung as fuel for cooking.

Shopping

Indians shop for fruit and vegetables in open-air markets. There are new shopping malls in big cities.

Young people enjoy shopping for clothes in malls.

Most shops are small. They do not have shop windows. Roadside stalls sell cheap goods or offer services, such as watch repairs.

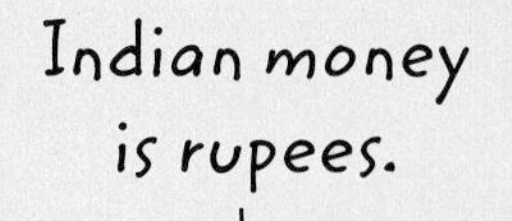
Indian money is rupees.

The shopkeepers open and close their shops when they want.

Food

In towns, people can buy all sorts of cheap, cooked snacks from street sellers.

You can buy roti bread with spicy vegetables from this street seller.

Most Indian meals include several dishes of spicy vegetables and sauces. These are served with bread or rice.

Indians make sweets from milk, flavoured with chocolate, coconut or nuts.

Some Indians eat at a table and use cutlery. Many eat sitting on the floor. They scoop up food with their right hand.

Sport and leisure

Cricket is the most popular sport in India. Boys play it on any open space they can find.

These boys play cricket on a crowded beach.

Indians enjoy watching films. Hundreds of films are made each year in Mumbai. The most popular films are musicals. They have lots of songs and dances.

There is always a wide choice of films to see at the cinema.

Holidays and festivals

There are many different religions in India. Most people are Hindus, but there are also Sikhs, Muslims, Buddhists and Christians.

Hindus pray in buildings called temples.

There are festivals throughout the year in India. Holi is a festival that celebrates the coming of spring. Diwali celebrates the Hindu New Year.

At Diwali, people light their homes with oil lamps and candles.

Speak Hindi!

Hindi is one of India's many languages. People use different Hindi words and speak with different accents depending on where they live in India.

Namaste (*Nah-mah-stay*)	Hello/ Goodbye
Kripya (*Krup-ya*)	Please
Shukriya (*Shook-ree-yah*)	Thank you
Haan (*Ha*)	Yes
Nahin (*N-he*)	No
Mera naam... hai (*Meh-ra nahm... hi*)	My name is ...

The Indian flag is always made from hand-spun cotton, silk or wool.

Indian Wildlife

India has several wildlife parks. Big animals, such as tigers, elephants and rhinoceroses, live there.

The tiger lives in dense forests and grasslands. It eats other animals, such as deer, goats and boar.

The Asian elephant wanders through forests. It eats grass, bark and leaves.

Make a collage of one of these animals.

Glossary

capital the city in a country where the government is

desert a place where it scarcely rains, so the earth is very dry and few plants can grow

fertile fertile land is good for growing food crops

festival a holiday when people celebrate something special

market a place with stalls where people buy and sell things

monsoon a time when heavy rain falls

plains a large flat area of land with few trees

season a particular time of the year

spice a plant that adds flavour to food

well a deep hole in the ground where people can get water

Index

Countries

Contents of titles in the series:

France 978 07502 6305 4

Where is France?
Land and Sea
The weather
Town and country
Homes
Shopping
Food
Sport
Holidays and festivals
Speak French!
Make a French flag
Glossary
Index

Poland 978 07502 6304 7

Where is Poland?
Land and Sea
The weather
Town and country
Homes
Shopping
Food
Sport
Religion and festivals
Speak Polish!
Make a Polish papercut
Glossary
Index

India 978 07502 6306 1

Where is India?
Land and Sea
The weather
Town and country
Homes
Shopping
Food
Sport and leisure
Holidays and festivals
Speak Hindi!
Indian wildlife
Glossary
Index

Spain 978 07502 6303 0

Where is Spain?
Land and Sea
The weather
Town and country
Homes
Shopping
Food
Sport
Holidays and festivals
Speak Spanish!
Play a Spanish game
Glossary
Index

WAYLAND

KE	12/10